then and now

NEVILLE
JOHNSON

SANGIN, THEN AND NOW

NEVILLE JOHNSON

DEAD RECKONING

20 17

COLLECTIVE

Copyright © 2023 Neville Johnson

Selected poems from this book were previously published in *War...
&After: The Anthology of Poet Warriors, Sweeping Leaves In The Wind, Alone
In A Crowded Room,* and *Good Soldiers Don't Cry*

Publisher: Dead Reckoning Collective
Editor: Keith Walter Dow
Book Cover Design: Tyler James Carroll & Keith Dow

Printed in the United States of America

ISBN-13: 979-8-9862724-4-3 (paperback)

CONTENTS

Homecoming

Making Sense

This book is dedicated to my children, Ruby, Aden, and Lexi.

And to my Mother.

"Glowing red hot hail rained down on our cold existence,

They welcomed us with a rage of burning bitter detestation."

-Neville Johnson

INTRODUCTION

My body went into a sensory overload as we slowly disappeared through pitch blackness, rapidly plunging into the mouth of hell. The overpowering roaring sound of the Chinook was deafening that night. That first step I took off the back of the tailgate was where it all began.

The months that followed in Sangin had a profound impact on me. I left a lot of me there when we departed the valley but brought back so much more. Writing this book was the release of post-war emotions and memories I chose to forget. It's my journey from then to now. Writing became my late-night companion, and this collection of poetry is a discovery of healing and a newfound passion for life.

HELMAND

ON ROUTE

Departed into the Helmand night.

Consumed by the Sangin Valley.

WELCOME!

The enemy greeted us with shrapnel,

Ripping up the earth,

Consuming us with fire.

Raging in, raining down,

From the jaws of Death,

Into the mouth of Hell.

HELMAND

By the old river

Beautiful Helmand Valley

Calm before the storm

DEPARTURE

They departed under the crescent howling moon,

Soft moonlight traveled through the night.

Bidding the dancing silhouettes farewell,

Their shadows consumed by the blackness.

Her pitch echoed well into the black burning night,

The distinctive roaring vibration hissed like an acoustic beast.

WAITING

Waiting, listening, and watching.

Observing, looking, and scanning.

Checking arcs, ears pinned back.

Waiting, knowing it's imminent.

Ready, finger on the trigger.

The deafening sound of Sangin town.

Heart beating; pounding hard.

RPG breaking the silence.

Squeezing the trigger, returning fire.

Tracers lighting the dawn.

A volley of thunder and Hell.

Sangin valley greeting the day.

SYMPHONY OF WAR

The music of war filled the air,

One by one, the song consumed us all.

Nature's sound hushed to a quiet,

As we prepared our orchestra.

We answered their call with our munitions composition,

Performing our symphony of war.

L7A2

Squeezing the trigger

GPMG ripping into the night

We are here to fight!

SUNSET

Sangin valley's sunset peace,

This foreign landscape, a thing of beauty.

A sunset I will remember,

My thoughts, my memories, beyond those hills.

Everything so insignificant,

Feeling calm,

Feeling content.

This moment doesn't last,

The sun burns out.

The night regains its throne,

Peace in the valley.

If only for a while.

1978

An old weathered photograph taken in 78,

Not long after my birth date.

My dear Mum gave it to me.

This one, you see, is one of a kind,

Taken in 78, in a place hard to find.

Grateful my Mum gave it to me.

The photograph discoloured and stained,

Time is deeply ingrained.

His memories of that day still remain.

QUIET TIMES

During the quiet times

My mind wanders

Thoughts drift

For a moment it felt real

It felt like home

I was home

For now, I'm here in the valley

I'm up, I'm moving

Running for cover

LANDSCAPE SOUND

The sounds of nature silenced,

My emotion toward nature, mutilated forever by this war.

No sounds of nature heard amid the drowning,

The endless pounding…

By these bombs.

Nature's sound died away to this distorted rage of bullets.

Helmand's sweet melody is replaced

By the sounds of the valley's gradual destruction.

We evolved at the same speed as

The forever metamorphosis of Sangin Town.

As the sound of guns began to be heard, I hear these enemies,

My new melodies.

The sound of nature subdued and replaced,

By the sound of war.

MIDNIGHT SCRIBBLES

Both death and life bowed their heads without hesitation,

Nodded and grinned with approval of the next existence.

These pages will take their time singing their bittersweet song,

Waiting in the shadows to speak their words.

My essence danced with the words,

And embraced each dying moment.

You will find it here,

Stories of yesteryear.

Before sun eludes night,

You will find me here, too.

STREETS

Broken mind, body, and soul.

Unforgiving Helmand heat.

Beauty beyond these Sangin streets.

RAINFALL

Awaiting the rising sun,
My gaze burning into the horizon.
Lost in the beauty of it all.

The wind blowing briskly and effortlessly,
The calm breeze reminding me,
You are here in the moment.
The old wind greets weathered sandbags,
Soothing the young souls.

No birds chirping, singing their song.
Rain soon to follow, heavy rain to fall.
Just like yesterday, and the day before.
Splash and splat!
Heavy rain falling all around us.
This rhythmic rain, tapping, tapping at our door.
Heavy hail falling, just like the other morning before,
Heavy pounding torrential downpour.
Heavy rainfall, oblivious to the life it takes.

The sounds of the heavens rapping,
Rapping at our door,
Chaotic drops falling, hitting hard.
Not slowing down for the impact of the ground.
Snapping bones, just like the day before.

Then, all is still.
Clear skies above, destruction below.
Heaviness to my coat today,
It was absent the day before.
More rain than predicted,
More rain to fall.
Just like yesterday, and the day before.

SANGIN

SANGIN NIGHTS

3 AM conversations

High on coffee

Low on life

Lucid dreaming

Magic wonder

Sangin nights

Seeing green

All can be seen

In the valley

The deafening sound of silence

LIFE

The life we take for granted,
So many things we take for granted.

Sitting here, reminiscing,
Contemplating my life.

Thinking and daydreaming,
Thoughts about returning home,
Lost track of the days.

Days with no names attached,
The unforgiving Helmand heat.

Sweat exuding through my pores,
I can hear the Sangin sound.

Talking to me, filling my mind,
These quiet moments breaking me.

Feelings difficult to describe,
Feeling tense, feeling tight.

Unable to relax,
God, I hate this feeling in me.

These quiet moments are breaking me,
Breaking me bit by bit.

Waiting for something to happen,
Reminiscing, contemplating,
Daydreaming, thinking.

These quiet moments,
Consuming me more and more.

STAIRWAY DOWN TO HEAVEN

The Depths of Heaven's dark dust-filled room.

Here you will find quietude amongst the smutted filled existence.

Down here, we have found shelter from the pain.

Here, at last, we have found peace…

Broken bodies, resting their souls here in oblivion.

The stairway up to Hell,

Awaits our return…

SANGIN RIVER

The constant flow of water disappears

Through a thick early morning haze.

The sound of the river sings beautiful, soulful blues.

The song of my soul is a song I need to hear.

Do I dare disturb this keeper of poetry?

I glance back as water flows under the bridge,

Like previous chapters flowing past,

Left smelling like musty water and faded memories.

EVOLVE

I'm him no more.

That version ceased to exist,

The loved one you once knew,

Evolved into something new,

Changed into something more.

A change of choice,

Essential to life.

ANXIETY

Days turn to nights, turn to days.

Eyes heavy and puffy, staring at the mirror with these eyes.

Night getting darker, the silence deafening at night.

Anxiety bleeding into my veins, feeding the anxiety.

This feeling I loathe, losing control, yet I know this.

Breathing deep, I must keep breathing!

Fight this, don't give up this fight!

NIGHTFALL

The Valley fell into a deep sleep when the guns fell silent.

An uncomfortable ghostly consciousness filled the air we breathed.

The life that surrounded us ceased to exist.

The symphony of birdsong departed this world.

MORNING ALARM

Quiet as we wait, we know it and we feel it.

It's in the air, it's near, and we sense it.

Waiting! Looking! Ready! Bring it!

RPG initiates the attack.

Squeezing the trigger, I answer the call.

My music of war.

These relentless attacks, raining in, burning down.

Not giving in, not giving up.

The hail of fire burning down.

These fuckers!

They're not giving up, not backing down.

The rounds keep raining,

We keep on fighting.

INSIDE THE WIRE

He came to visit once more,

Tapping, rapping at our door.

His smell lingered around.

I was still, utterly still.

He was stalking the valley once more.

This odious, faceless shadow,

With no mercy or kindness.

A morbid nothingness,

There was no heart to beat in his chest,

A black void filling the space.

Nor tears to shed from his black sockets.

Death lingered inside the wire,

His silence burned us all.

Ripping away a part of me, part of us all.

The hooded vale of Death had covered this Valley,

Smothering us all.

120

Dilated pupils.

My adrenaline pumping.

Close call incoming.

SMOKING

A drag calms me.

My heart pumps, racing hard.

This heightened state, such a rush.

We take turns in drags

Filling us, calming us, breathing in deep.

The relentless enemy, walking the rounds,

Walking the rounds, walking them in.

Danger close they fall, one by one.

Taking a drag, calming my nerves.

My rapid breathing, slowing down.

Breathing deep, filling my lungs.

I hear them fall, hitting the earth with a thud.

Louder and louder with each impact.

Closer and closer they crawl.

Rounds falling hard, raining down.

Walking the rounds, walking them in.

BENEATH THE VISITING MOON

In search of war, the boys smiling like never before.

One by one into the early haze they disappear.

Boys return as men, faces telling stories of waging war.

For these men, there is nothing left so glorious,

Beneath the visiting moon.

AFTERMATH

At night that unusual feeling comes to me,

Quivering in the darkness.

That odd strangeness,

The Valley hums with the cries

Of the long dead souls,

Bending my ear in the night,

In the Graveyard of Empires.

LAST PATROL

My war is over.

Feeling empty.

Feeling numb.

My war is over.

It's fucking done.

No joy,

Nor sadness.

Neither contentment,

Nor despair.

Unable to think,

Unable to feel.

A void filling

My empty soul.

Filling to the brim,

Empty vessel overflowing.

I'M READY

No more fear.

My time came to an end.

Mission over, mission done.

My last footprint stamped in the Sangin sand.

Tired body and exhausted soul.

Sleeplessness, my companion no more.

My face and hands, caked in dirt.

My eyes tell a tale.

My Sangin Valley tale

I am drained of strength.

Some days, only but a blur.

I gaze into nothing.

My thousand yard stare.

I am ready here,

Take me home.

Take me, please.

THESE EYES

My tired eyes,

Hiding my cries.

My dreadful disguise,

Hiding behind these eyes.

I despise my dust-filled cries.

My tired eyes,

My life flickers and dies.

Giving in led to my demise,

No more sun in my eyes,

My last Sangin sunrise.

THE VALLEY

I gave a piece of me away,

I took a piece of you away.

The pieces that remain

Decay.

A piece of me, I gave away,

A piece of you, I took away.

Some of me died

That day.

PARTED WAYS

That day we parted ways.

That was the last of what I saw of him,

The last of what he saw of me.

Forever changed, never the same.

HOMECOMING

HOMECOMING

Dimly lit empty room,

My life in boxes.

Alone in my room,

Edge of my bed.

I can feel the void,

Weighing me down.

The overwhelming feeling,

My bittersweet ending.

I'm sobbing and crying,

Empty void overflowing.

Silence taking hold,

White noise fills my mind.

Laughter breaking the silence,

I'm laughing and crying.

I realize I made it,

I'm home.

I MISS

Miss the warm days.

Miss the Sangin days.

The lads, the good times.

Miss the banter.

The lads, the brothers.

Miss what we had.

The brotherhood,

That was us, the lads.

I miss the 3 AM conversations.

We had it every day.

I miss them today.

Missing the time,

When days feel grey.

INK

Engraved in my skin.

Imprinted in my mind,

Burned into my soul.

Forgotten for a while,

Until now.

MEMORIES OF WAR

Words flow and fall.

I can write, just pour me more.

Thoughts and feelings return.

My memories of war.

Memories pouring, flooding in.

A distant life, I live no more.

I need to write, pour me more.

A time, a place forgotten.

My thoughts of post-war,

I need to write to remember.

My memories of war,

Not just a dying ember.

Pour me some more.

SANGIN

Sangin days,

Sangin nights.

Some days I remember.

Some days I choose to forget.

Other days I can't help but miss

Sangin town,

My wonderful wild.

AFTERMATH

The darker residue of our previous lives stored away,

Keeping the darkness at bay.

In quiet moments I hear past conversations and jokes,

Stories told with a dark sense of humour.

But at night, I sense that unusual feeling,

A quiver in the darkness, that odd strangeness.

The Valley hums with the cries of the long-dead souls.

It forces my ear to the night.

THESE ENEMIES

My memory of memories,

They swim and flow, these enemies.

My distant dark stories,

Drowning in these memories.

STRANGER TO MYSELF

What have I become?

A stranger to many.

A stranger to myself.

Looking in the mirror.

I see him staring at me.

I can't find me in there.

I don't recognize him.

How long have you been here?

Completely unknown to myself.

Engulfed in numbness to all.

Who is this old man I see?

Grey hair, wrinkled face.

I see the rage in his eyes.

Anger in his soul.

Do I know you?

Looking through me.

Staring at nothing.

Who have I become?

What have I become?

A stranger to all.

TIME

Moving along gently.

Creeping through slowly.

Ticking away quietly.

This man-made construct

Slowly burning out.

My own time

Slowly running out.

Advice from my father:

"Do not waste time, my son

Live life with purpose.

Time you waste you will never get back.

Please, my son, listen to me.

Learn from my mistakes,

Take my advice,

My time, your time

All the time we have is what we think.

Truth is, we don't!

My time, your time,

All down to the nanosecond.

My son, learn from me.

Fight! Fight the ticking clock!"

FATHER AND SON

Those days, long gone now;

Nothing more than a recollection.

The conversations went silent.

Our silence speaks a thousand tears.

Wars in foreign lands.

We walk the same path apart,

We feel the same pain together.

IN SEARCH OF WAR

This boy followed you to no man's land,

He dreamt of Ovamboland.

This boy followed the spoor left by you,

He followed you to war.

From boy to man, to war, to peace,

Lost and alone.

Fragments of me, of you, I see.

This boy followed you to war.

Now I stand alone amongst many,

I stand still and they move to and fro.

Feeling numb amidst this resonant noise,

Free falling I fall, amongst this scattering mess

I still dream of you, of war.

Dreams of Ovamboland, our no man's land.

Stranded in this wasteland,

My old man, sitting on the white sand.

I followed you to war.

MY QUINTESSENCE

Without realizing I have subconsciously gone away.
Pushed people away from me, away from it all.
Gradually creating the void between the world and me.
Digging away at my trench more each day and night.
Escaping deeper with every inch, I orchestrated.
Moving me further from humanity.
My inner voice begging to stop.

Deep in me in my depth of what I have become.
I accept it all.
I acknowledge it is me.
For I don't blame them, nor you.
I chose this desolate existence.

In the quiet depth I constructed, I hear her voice.
Her gentle voice so ever soft.
A kind-hearted voice in a deafening world.
Her voice illuminated the destructive numbness.
Burned the haze of my essence.

The voice saved a life I chose back then.
She guided me to where I belonged.
I accepted, but not out of wanting.
It was a necessity for me.
She is my quintessence of life.

MIDNIGHT SCREAMS

The night is a special kind of black.

It's the kind I want to clutch.

Night comes as a reward of sorts.

A quiet above to calm the anger below.

WHAT IF

What if I never left in June?

What if I never boarded the flight?

What if I never felt the desire?

No will, no ambition.

What if I had a different dream?

What if I was there instead of here?

What if I never served the Queen?

No God, nor country.

What if I never met the valley?

What if I never experienced fear?

What if my hands never felt the cold steel?

ANGER

Gut-wrenching, upturning feeling,
Breathing deep to release it.
Trying to focus on each breath,
Attempting to focus on something else.

This feeling I hate the most,
Trying to keep my mind busy,
Maybe if I'm distracted it will fade away,
Refuse to look it in the eye,
Aggression's dark desire to take control.

Anger bleeding into my veins,
Internal struggle in my mind,
Struggle to control my breathing,
Anxiety boiling filling my gut,
Slowly taking over taking control.

Clenching my fists I stand up.
Resisting fighting, not giving up.
Out of the shadow, she appears.

Placing her hand on my shoulder,
Her soft voice killing the white noise.
Seeing the hope in her eyes,
You can fight this,
We can stop this.

Her voice of hope for my soul,
Anxiety slowly dying away.
My angel, my savior,
Not leaving my side.

MAKING SENSE

STILL

These quiet moments

Seem so loud!

KIRITUHI

My beautiful but ferocious chapter,

Twisted and turned,

But carried on,

A journey carved in black ink.

A visual account of joy and happiness,

Telling a story of utter desolation and pain.

A new awakening with new life, harmony,

Peace and tranquillity scarred in flesh.

ANOTHER DAY

Nature's sound subdued to a whisper;

A heaviness to my soul today.

It was absent the day before;

Her exquisite glow illuminates my grey existence.

Her golden vibrant rays

Give bright color to the clouds and mountains,

Filling the sky with shades of pink, peach, and amber.

Colors, so gentle for the soul.

She brings hope of a new beginning,

Just like yesterday,

And the day before.

She will bring the same tomorrow,

Hope for all.

And yet, the valley remains dark and meaningless.

DAYDREAMING

As I close my eyes I drift to that place.

The smell, the sound so reverberating.

The distinctive roaring vibration.

Sound of hope.

Dust covered faces and hands caked in blood.

The smiles on their faces.

Death behind those eyes.

Oh, those eyes,

Cold death-filled eyes.

Oh, those eyes.

DAYS END

Mesmerizing cool soft evening colors,

Taking her dark secrets away with her.

And rise she will again.

And rise she will again.

MORE OF THE SAME

Another day, just like yesterday.

Like the day before it.

Days rolling through, days with no name.

Night turns to day, burns to night.

Time burns on, burns out.

This manmade construct.

These days have a hold, holding back.

They are moving, I'm standing still.

Still, I stand amongst these mountains,

Been here long before me, will remain long after I depart.

Turns, burns to dust.

Another day tomorrow,

The way today burns to dust.

HISTORY OF VIOLENCE

Staring back reminds me of what hurts.

Looking back upon a life once lived.

I feel like a worn-out book without a warm touch.

This old, heavy, dusty book,

Soft leather, hard interior.

Looking back at past chapters, words appear and disappear,

My heavy eyes stare at these worn and torn pages.

A mountain of pages, as old as time.

Black ink pressed into the aged innards.

A few pages ripped out, discarded by the roadside.

This leatherbound book speaks volumes,

My written history of violence.

SLEEPLESSNESS

Late night reflections,

There is no need for introductions.

We are just shadows,

Blending into the dark.

Glowing embers leaping,

Rhythmic flames twirling.

Hot wick flickering,

Burning in an incandescent dance.

MY DEAR CHILD

My dear child,

You remind me to pause,

To celebrate the evanescence of the present.

The wonder of now,

My current time and place in this life.

My dear child,

You remind me to embrace this,

All the exaltation of the present moment.

MY ROAD

The road I wanted to walk as a child.

The path I dreamt of exploring since 1978.

The road I longed for, the road not traveled.

The road that my love and passion called for.

The road I stumbled on as a child that made me a man.

The road that lost me.

The road that found me.

The road I followed to war.

The road I explored alone that I left my footprints on.

The road that broke me, healed me, scarred my soul.

The road that gave me courage, hope, and love.

The road I followed you on.

TIME TO THINK

This painful demise, it's no surprise.

These memories, my enemies,

They swim and flow, hiding behind these eyes.

My self-created orchestrated melodies,

The lyrics fill the void.

My dark, musical composition, my own creation,

My complete existence feels destroyed.

In the end, my complete black annihilation.

WORDS LESS WRITTEN

These days the drums beat a slower, quiet rhythm,

Without missing a beat, this book has been altered by time.

With black ink bleeding into new space,

Words appear, and with time they fade.

The room resounds to the sound of my words,

And covers me in moon dust.

The waxing crescent moon gazing down,

Appears to approve of these old dark tales.

ADEN

I remember that it hurt

you more.

I remember that you needed me

more than before.

I failed you in a time of need.

I failed you as a father.

You deserve better,

Not a stranger.

My son, be better.

My son, be more.

DONE

History is set in stone,

My story has been told.

It's your turn, my son.

Write your story.

Tell your tale.

Write what you know.

ACKNOWLEDGEMENTS

My greatest appreciation is for my wife, Stephanie Johnson.

You've given me the courage to be something I never thought I'd be, a writer.

Previously Published Works by Dead Reckoning Collective:

Fact & Memory by: Tyler Carroll & Keith Dow

In Love… &War: The Poet Warrior Anthology Vol. 1

War… &After: The Poet Warrior Anthology Vol. 2

war{n}pieces by: Leo Jenkins

Lucky Joe by: Brian Kimber, Leo Jenkins, and David Rose

Sober Man's Thoughts by: William Bolyard

Karmic Purgatory by: Keith Dow

War is a Racket by: Smedley Butler

The First Marauder by: Luke Ryan

Where They Meet by: Cokie

Poppies by: Amy Sexaur

Rock Eater by: Mason Rodrigue

Revision of a Man by: Matt Smythe

On Assimilation by: Leo Jenkins

Upcoming Publications by Dead Reckoning Collective:

A Word Like God by: Leo Jenkins

Phantoms by: Ben Fortier

Carmen Et Error by: Moises Machuca

DEAD RECKONING COLLECTIVE

COLLECTIVE

DEAD RECKONING COLLECTIVE is a veteran owned and operated publishing company. Our mission encourages literacy as a component of a positive lifestyle. Although DRC only publishes the written work of military veterans, the intention of closing the divide between civilians and veterans is held in the highest regard. By sharing these stories it is our hope that we can help to clarify how veterans should be viewed by the public and how veterans should view themselves.

Visit us at:

deadreckoningco.com

@deadreckoningcollective

@deadreckoningco

@DRCpublishing

Sangin, Then and Now is Neville Johnson's first published collection of poetry.

His writing has previously appeared in:

War... &After: The Anthology of Poet Warriors

Sweeping Leaves In The Wind

Alone In A Crowded Room

Good Soldiers Don't Cry

Follow NEVILLE JOHNSON

 @nevillejohnson01

NEVILLE JOHNSON was born and raised in South Africa by a Mum who was a Nurse and a Dad who was a Police Officer. This early exposure to a life of service to country influenced his most significant life decisions. Before he started writing, this path took him to the United Kingdom, where he ended up in London as a member of her Majesty's Royal Infantry.

Neville currently resides in New Zealand with his wife and three children. He works at a high school as the Pathways Coordinator, assisting young people in developing essential life skills for their transition into the workforce.

CPSIA information can be obtained
at www.ICGtesting.com
Printed in the USA
BVHW041158080223
658123BV00023B/399